U.S. Government Q&A!

What Is the PRESIDENTIAL LINE OF SUCCESSION?

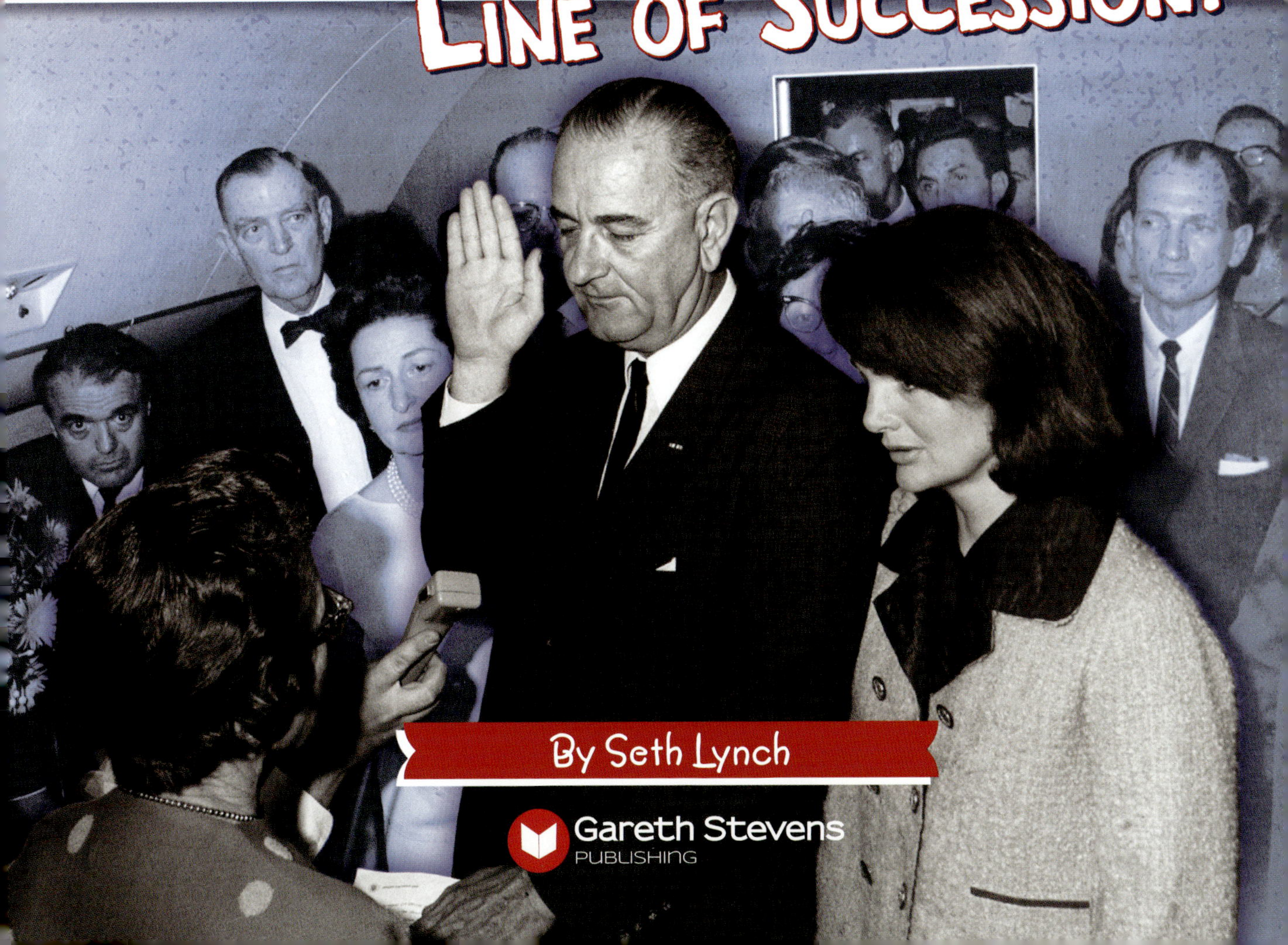

By Seth Lynch

Gareth Stevens PUBLISHING

Please visit our website, www.garethstevens.com. For a free color catalog of all our high-quality books, call toll free 1-800-542-2595 or fax 1-877-542-2596.

Library of Congress Cataloging-in-Publication Data
Names: Lynch, Seth, author.
Title: What is the presidential line of succession? / Seth Lynch.
Description: Buffalo : Gareth Stevens Publishing, 2026. | Series: U.s. government q & a! | Includes index. | Audience: Grades 2-3
Identifiers: LCCN 2024045551 (print) | LCCN 2024045552 (ebook) | ISBN 9781482470116 (library binding) | ISBN 9781482470109 (paperback) | ISBN 9781482470123 (ebook)
Subjects: LCSH: Presidents–Succession–United States–History–Juvenile literature. | United States. Constitution. 25th Amendment–Juvenile literature. | Federal government–United States–Juvenile literature.
Classification: LCC KF5082 .L96 2026 (print) | LCC KF5082 (ebook) | DDC 342.73/062–dc23/eng/20241026
LC record available at https://lccn.loc.gov/2024045551
LC ebook record available at https://lccn.loc.gov/2024045552

First Edition

Published in 2026 by
Gareth Stevens Publishing
2544 Clinton Street
Buffalo, NY 14224

Designer: Andrea Davison-Bartolotta
Editor: Kristen Nelson

Photo credits: Cover, pp. 1, 13 LBJ Library photo by Cecil Stoughton; series art (paper, feather) Incomible/Shutterstock.com; series art (blue banner, red banner, stars) pingbat/Shutterstock.com; pp. 5 (both), 7, 11, 12, 18, 19 courtesy of Library of Congress; p. 15 Andrew Leyden/Shutterstock.com; p. 17 (left) File:25th Amendment Pg1of2 AC.jpg/Wikimedia Commons; p. 17 (right) File:25th Amendment Pg2of2 AC.jpg/Wikimedia Commons.

Printed in the United States of America

CPSIA compliance information: Batch #CSGS26: For further information contact Gareth Stevens, New York, New York at 1-800-542-2595.

Contents

Words in the glossary appear in **bold** type the first time they are used in the text.

The Tyler Precedent

In 1841, William Henry Harrison became the first U.S. president to die while in office. Harrison's vice president, John Tyler, was soon sworn in to succeed, or follow, Harrison as U.S. president. This move set a **precedent** for the presidential line of succession going forward.

The U.S. president leads the U.S. government. They carry out laws made by Congress. The president is commander in chief of the armed forces too. What happens today when such an important person can't lead?

Government Guides

Congress is the part of the U.S. government made up of the Senate and the House of **Representatives**.

William Henry Harrison

John Tyler

Not everyone agreed that Tyler became the president upon Harrison's death. Some thought he should be called the "acting" president and only hold office until a special **election** could be held.

What Is It?

The presidential line of succession is the list of people who would become the president if the president dies, resigns, is removed from office, or is **incapacitated**. The idea of a line of succession is part of the U.S. Constitution, the highest law in the United States.

The Constitution says that if the president cannot finish their term, the vice president takes on the job. There aren't many **details**, however. For example, the Constitution doesn't say who would then become vice president!

Government Guides

To resign means to choose to leave office.

The Constitution originally didn't say who would decide a president was too incapacitated to serve. President Dwight D. Eisenhower, shown here, had a heart attack in 1955. At the time, it was unclear who would make the call that someone needed to step in as president.

Succession Laws

The first law addressing the presidential line of succession was passed in 1792. It said if the president and vice president could not serve as president, the president pro tempore of the Senate was next in line. The Speaker of the House of Representatives would be after that.

An 1886 law changed this. It made the secretary of state the first in line to the presidency after the vice president. Other members of the president's cabinet followed in the order their department, or office, was created.

Who Are They?

president pro tempore of the Senate

the senator who leads the Senate when the vice president is not present

Speaker of the House of Representatives

the person chosen by a vote in the House to lead the official duties of the House

cabinet

a group of senior officials appointed by the president as special advisors. They lead departments such as homeland security, education, and energy, and are each called "secretary" of that department.

Aside from the vice president, none of the leaders in the line of succession set up by the laws in 1792 and 1886 were elected by the American people.

Truman's Law

In 1945, President Franklin D. Roosevelt died in office. Vice President Harry Truman became president. Truman believed people who were elected to their office should be near the top in the order of succession. He pushed for yet another law to change the line of succession.

The Presidential Succession Act of 1947 put the Speaker of the House next in line after the vice president. The president pro tempore of the Senate became third in the order of succession. The secretary of state was fourth.

Government Guides

Truman said the Speaker of the House was the leader of representatives chosen by the American people and that's why this person should be third in line.

President Harry Truman, shown here, was good friends with the Speaker of the House. That's likely why that position was put ahead of the president pro tempore of the Senate in the order of succession in 1947.

Big Changes

Not long after the third law about presidential succession passed, a bigger change was brought up: an amendment to the Constitution.

The idea came about during President Eisenhower's time in office from 1953 to 1961. He fell very ill several times. Then, President John F. Kennedy was **assassinated** in 1963. Congress began to push for a clearer line of succession. It wanted official rules of what to do if the president couldn't lead for some reason—and how to fill the **role** of vice president.

John F. Kennedy

Vice President Lyndon Johnson was sworn in as president about two hours after President Kennedy died.

Government Guides

An amendment is a change to the U.S. Constitution. Because it's part of the Constitution, it supersedes, or takes the place of, laws that may have come before it.

The 25th Amendment

The 25th Amendment went into effect in 1967. Its first section, or part, says the vice president officially becomes president should the president die, resign, or be removed from office. The second section says this new president will **nominate** a new vice president. Congress has to agree to the person filling the vice presidency.

The amendment's third part allows the vice president to take on the role of acting president for a time. This happens if the president is sick, hurt, or otherwise incapacitated.

Government Guides

Before the amendment passed, some presidents and their vice presidents agreed on what to do should the president become sick or unable to lead for some reason.

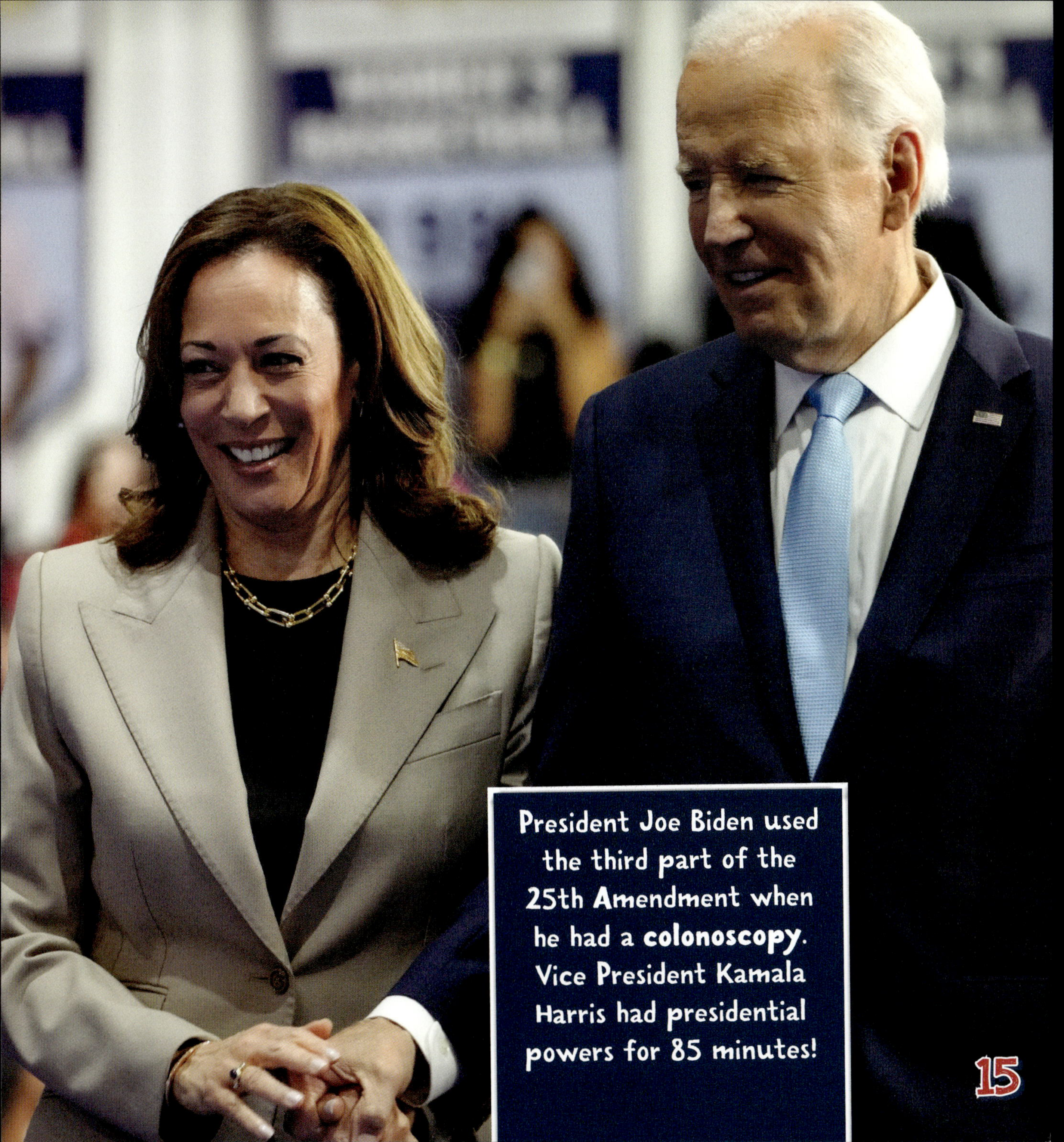

President Joe Biden used the third part of the 25th Amendment when he had a **colonoscopy**. Vice President Kamala Harris had presidential powers for 85 minutes!

Section Four

The fourth section of the 25th Amendment sets up who can say a president is too incapacitated to serve. It is the vice president and cabinet members, or another group Congress decides. Should this happen, the vice president takes on the president's role.

This section also says how a president can come back after **recovering**. It sets up rules for the vice president and cabinet to **dispute** the president's ability to come back too. As of 2024, the fourth section of the 25th Amendment has never been used.

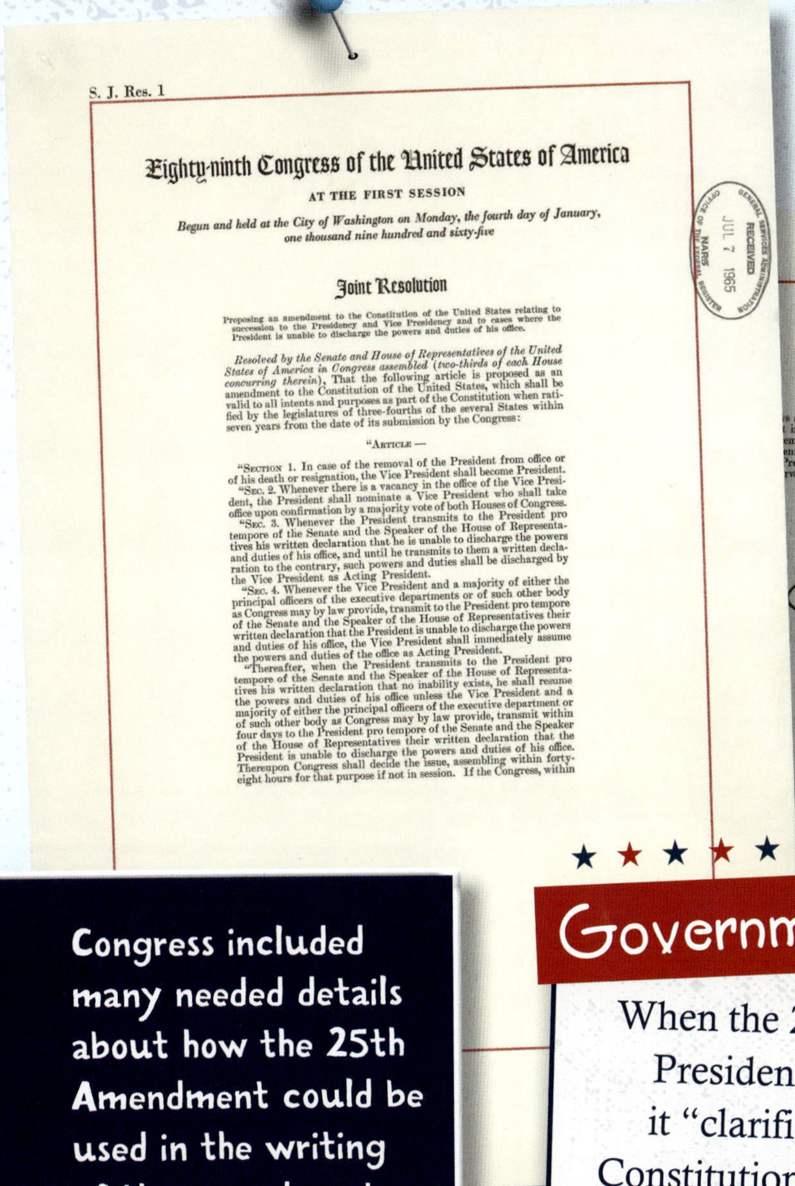

S. J. Res. 1

Eighty-ninth Congress of the United States of America

AT THE FIRST SESSION

Begun and held at the City of Washington on Monday, the fourth day of January, one thousand nine hundred and sixty-five

Joint Resolution

Proposing an amendment to the Constitution of the United States relating to succession to the Presidency and Vice Presidency and to cases where the President is unable to discharge the powers and duties of his office.

Resolved by the Senate and House of Representatives of the United States of America in Congress assembled (two-thirds of each House concurring therein), That the following article is proposed as an amendment to the Constitution of the United States, which shall be valid to all intents and purposes as part of the Constitution when ratified by the legislatures of three-fourths of the several States within seven years from the date of its submission by the Congress:

"Article —

"Section 1. In case of the removal of the President from office or of his death or resignation, the Vice President shall become President.

"Sec. 2. Whenever there is a vacancy in the office of the Vice President, the President shall nominate a Vice President who shall take office upon confirmation by a majority vote of both Houses of Congress.

"Sec. 3. Whenever the President transmits to the President pro tempore of the Senate and the Speaker of the House of Representatives his written declaration that he is unable to discharge the powers and duties of his office, and until he transmits to them a written declaration to the contrary, such powers and duties shall be discharged by the Vice President as Acting President.

"Sec. 4. Whenever the Vice President and a majority of either the principal officers of the executive departments or of such other body as Congress may by law provide, transmit to the President pro tempore of the Senate and the Speaker of the House of Representatives their written declaration that the President is unable to discharge the powers and duties of his office, the Vice President shall immediately assume the powers and duties of the office as Acting President.

"Thereafter, when the President transmits to the President pro tempore of the Senate and the Speaker of the House of Representatives his written declaration that no inability exists, he shall resume the powers and duties of his office unless the Vice President and a majority of either the principal officers of the executive department or of such other body as Congress may by law provide, transmit within four days to the President pro tempore of the Senate and the Speaker of the House of Representatives their written declaration that the President is unable to discharge the powers and duties of his office. Thereupon Congress shall decide the issue, assembling within forty-eight hours for that purpose if not in session. If the Congress, within

S. J. Res. 1—2

s after receipt of the latter written declaration, or, if
t in session, within twenty-one days after Congress is
emble, determines by two-thirds vote of both Houses
ent is unable to discharge the powers and duties of his
President shall continue to discharge the same as Acting
rwise, the President shall resume the powers and duties

Speaker of the House of Representatives.

Vice President of the United States and President of the Senate.

Congress included many needed details about how the 25th Amendment could be used in the writing of the amendment.

Government Guides

When the 25th Amendment passed, President Lyndon Johnson said it "clarifies," or makes clear, the Constitution's words about succession and filling the role of vice president.

Amendment in Action

In 1973, Vice President Spiro Agnew resigned. At the time, he was being **investigated** for several crimes. President Richard Nixon used the 25th Amendment to nominate a new vice president. Gerald Ford was a congressman in the House of Representatives at the time. Less than two months after Agnew stepped down, Ford became vice president.

In 1974, President Nixon also resigned. He, too, was being investigated for wrongdoing. Gerald Ford became president on August 9, 1974!

Richard Nixon

To date, Gerald Ford is the only U.S. president to hold office without having been elected either president or vice president.

The Line Today

The vice president gets the most attention when discussing the line of succession. However, there is a list of offices that follow the vice president in the line of succession today! The secretary of veterans affairs and secretary of homeland security have been added to this list most recently.

The presidential line of succession hasn't always been clear. But history shows that in order to keep the United States running, clarity of this line is of great importance!

Think About It!

Cabinet members are not elected by the people, but chosen by the president. Does it make sense for them to be in the line of succession to the presidency? Why or why not?

The Presidential Line of Succession

- vice president
- Speaker of the House
- president pro tempore of the Senate
- secretary of state
- secretary of the treasury
- secretary of defense
- attorney general
- secretary of the interior
- secretary of agriculture
- secretary of commerce
- secretary of labor
- secretary of health and human services
- secretary of housing and urban development
- secretary of transportation
- secretary of energy
- secretary of education
- secretary of veterans affairs
- secretary of homeland security

If the president dies, resigns, or is incapacitated in some way, this is the order of who would become president.

Glossary

assassinate: To kill someone, especially a public figure.

colonoscopy: The medical procedure when a doctor uses tools to look in someone's colon.

detail: A small part of something.

dispute: To say something is not correct or true.

election: The act of voting someone into a government position.

incapacitated: Having to do with being unable or unfit to move or work as one usually does.

investigate: To try to find out the facts about something, such as a crime.

nominate: To suggest someone for a job.

precedent: Something done or said in the past that sets a model for the future.

recover: To get better after an illness.

representative: A member of a lawmaking body who acts for voters.

role: The part that one plays in a job or community.

For More Information

Books

Faust, Daniel R. *The Electoral College.* Minneapolis, MN: Bearport Publishing, 2022.

Finn, Peter. *Electing the Vice President.* Buffalo, NY: Cavendish Square Publishing, 2025.

McKinney, Donna B. *The Presidents Encyclopedia.* Minneapolis, MN: Encyclopedias, an imprint of Abdo Reference, 2023.

Websites

About the Vice President
https://www.senate.gov/about/officers-staff/vice-president.htm
Find out more about the vice president's part in the U.S. government here.

Kids in the House
https://kids-clerk.house.gov/young-learners/
Use the House of Representatives website for kids to learn more about the U.S. government.

The Executive Branch
https://www.ducksters.com/history/us_executive_branch.php
Learn more about what the U.S. president does here.

Publisher's note to educators and parents: Our editors have carefully reviewed these websites to ensure that they are suitable for students. Many websites change frequently, however, and we cannot guarantee that a site's future contents will continue to meet our high standards of quality and educational value. Be advised that students should be closely supervised whenever they access the internet.

Index